Coffee Traditions
AROUND THE WORLD

This book belongs to:

____

BIBI LEBLANC

First Edition
Printed in the United States of America

ISBN 978-1-959924-50-0

Cover Design & Illustrations by Culture to Color® LLC
Text by Bibi LeBlanc

For more information, visit
CultureToColor.com

Order in bulk or custom-brand your own Explainer Book™:
CS@CultureToColor.com
386-228-5147

Contact the Author
bibi@culturetocolor.com
386-228-5147
LinkedIn: linkedin.com/in/bibileblanc

WELCOME

... TO THE WORLD IN MY COFFEE CUP

I have always believed that coffee is never just coffee.
It is the scent of roasted beans drifting through an open window. The sound of
spoons against porcelain. The quiet moment before the day begins. The long
conversation that stretches far beyond the last sip.

As I began exploring coffee traditions around the world, I realized
that every cup tells a story. In some places, coffee is a ceremony.
In others, it is a quick pause at a busy counter. Sometimes, it is sweet and spiced,
other times dark and bold, but everywhere it carries culture, memory,
and connection.

This book is my invitation to you: travel through coffee rituals, history,
and everyday moments, and add your own color along the way.

Take your time.
Imagine the sounds, the smells, the people.
Let each page feel like sitting down for coffee together.

With a love for coffee from my home to yours,

Bibi Le Blanc

*P.S. I would love to see your colored pages. Please share your colored creations
with me at bibi@culturetocolor.com*
Seeing your interpretations brings these traditions
to life in the most beautiful way.

COLOMBIA
Coffee And The Mountain

Morning mist lifts slowly from the hills.

Rows of coffee plants trace the slopes, their glossy leaves catching the early morning light as the day begins. Red cherries are picked by hand, one by one, carried in woven baskets down narrow paths.

Harvesting is careful work. Only ripe cherries are selected. The beans are washed, fermented, dried in the sun, and sorted with practiced attention. Entire regions depend on this rhythm. Families return to the fields season after season.

Coffee here is both livelihood and legacy.

Small farms cling to steep terrain. Conversations happen while sorting beans. Generations learn the feel of ripeness between their fingers. The work is steady and precise.

Later, when the coffee is brewed, its flavor carries notes shaped by the altitude and the soil. Coffee remains central to rural communities, shaping both economy and identity.

Coffee arrived in Colombia in the 18th century and gradually spread across the Andean highlands. By the 19th century, it had become one of the country's most important exports. Colombian coffee is known worldwide for its quality and distinct regional profiles.

ETHIOPIA
WHERE COFFEE WAS FIRST SHARED

Smoke rises slowly from a small charcoal stove. Green coffee beans crackle as they darken, their scent drifting outward, filling the room before the first word is spoken.

In Ethiopia, the ceremony begins with washing the beans, then roasting them carefully over an open flame. Guests are invited to inhale the aroma as it rises. It is a gesture that signals the gathering has begun. The roasted beans are ground by hand with a mortar and pestle, the rhythmic sound steady and familiar. Water heats in a clay pot called a *jebena*.
When the coffee is ready, it is poured in three rounds.

The first cup is strong.
The second softens.
The third blesses.

Time stretches differently here; coffee is not a quick pause in the day. Neighbors sit close. Elders speak. Children play nearby. The ceremony can last hours, not because it is slow, but because it carries meaning. Coffee marks reconciliation, celebration, welcome, and remembrance.

It is the structure around which the day gathers. The ritual protects something precious: presence.

Legend tells of a goat herder named Kaldi who noticed his goats dancing after eating red berries. Monks roasted the berries and brewed a drink that helped them stay awake during prayer.

ITALY
ESPRESSO AND THE BAR

The cup is small. The counter is crowded.

An espresso arrives in seconds, placed on a saucer with practiced ease. No one settles into a chair. Most stand. A quick nod to the barista. A coin left beside the register.

In Italy, coffee is brief but exact.

Espresso is taken at the bar, often in a single sip. Cappuccino belongs to the morning. After midday, it is espresso again. Orders are simple and specific. The crema should be smooth. The temperature just right. There is no rush, even in the speed of the serving.

Regulars greet one another. The barista remembers names. Newspapers are folded under arms. The exchange is efficient but familiar. The ritual happens daily, sometimes several times a day. Coffee does not stretch the afternoon here. It punctuates it.

Here, espresso marks time in small, steady pauses.

A SIP OF HISTORY

Coffee arrived in Italy through trade routes in the 16th century and quickly became part of public life. Venice was among the first European cities to open coffeehouses. Over time, Italy refined the espresso machine, transforming how coffee was brewed and served.

Today, the Italian espresso bar remains a defining feature of daily life, where speed and precision coexist with tradition.

TURKEY
COFFEE AND THE ART OF THE POUR

The foam rises slowly in the *cezve*, a small, long-handled pot. Finely ground coffee simmers over low heat, watched carefully so it does not spill. Timing matters.

In Turkey, coffee is prepared with attention. Water and coffee are heated together, sometimes sweetened before brewing. When the foam forms, it is spooned gently into small, delicate cups before the rest is poured. Guests sit close to the table. Conversation begins only after the first sip.

When the coffee is finished, the cup may be turned upside down onto its saucer.
The coffee grounds slide and settle into patterns, a stage that gives rise to one of the most unique traditions: fortune-telling by reading the patterns in the leftover grounds.
Someone lifts the cup and studies the shapes left behind. The reading becomes part of the visit, less prediction than shared reflection.

Here, coffee is a symbol of culture, connection, and contemplation. It is a drink that invites conversation, observation, and even a little mystery.

Coffee reached the Ottoman Empire in the 16th century and quickly spread through Istanbul's coffeehouses. These spaces became centers of social and political life so influential that rulers occasionally attempted to restrict them. The bans never lasted. Turkish coffee endured and is now recognized by UNESCO as part of the country's intangible cultural heritage.*

*The Ottoman Empire was a vast imperial power that lasted from the late 13th century until 1922. With its capital in Istanbul, it reached its height and controlled large parts of Southeast Europe, the Middle East, and North Africa.

AUSTRIA
COFFEE AND THE WIENER KAFFEEHAUS

Austria's coffee culture is inseparable from the *Viennese Kaffeehaus*.

These cafés are not simply places to drink coffee. They are spaces where time is intentionally unhurried. Patrons settle in to read, write, observe, or sit quietly for hours, without expectation or pressure.

Historically, the coffeehouse welcomed writers, musicians, and political thinkers. Newspapers lay within reach. Conversations rose and fell naturally. Solitude and debate shared the same room. Coffee arrived with care, often accompanied by a pastry, reminding guests that the experience mattered as much as the drink.

Unlike faster café cultures, the Viennese coffeehouse values continuity. Guests return to the same tables again and again. The space becomes familiar. Known.

The *Kaffeehaus* is a public living room, open to all. In Austria, coffee is a companion to reflection. The coffeehouse endures because it protects something rare: the freedom to linger.

Vienna's café culture traces back to the late 17th century, when coffeehouses began appearing after the Ottoman presence in the region. Over time, these cafés became gathering places for writers, musicians, and political thinkers.
Figures such as Freud and Trotsky once sat beneath high ceilings at marble tables.

Today, Viennese Kaffeehaus culture is recognized by UNESCO as part of Austria's cultural heritage, preserving not just a drink, but a way of spending time.

WIENER
KAFFEE

VIETNAM
PHIN BREWING AND SWEET PATIENCE

The drip is slow. Dark coffee filters through a small metal *phin*, falling steadily into a layer of condensed milk. Drop by deliberate drop. Coffee is built in layers.

The brew is strong, often made from robusta beans. Bitter coffee meets thick sweetness at the bottom of the glass. When the filter is lifted, the two are stirred together until the colors blend into caramel brown.

Ice often waits nearby. The contrast is part of the pleasure: hot and cold, bitter and sweet, dense and refreshing.

Watching the drip becomes part of the experience. Conversations unfold at low tables. Scooters pass in the background. Regulars return to the same corner cafés each morning. Coffee here is not hurried. It is allowed to complete its process.

Whether served hot or poured over ice, coffee is not just brewed. It unfolds. Each cup invites calm, focus, and quiet enjoyment.

A SIP OF HISTORY

In 1940s Hanoi, fresh milk was scarce. A creative bartender whisked egg yolks with sugar and poured the mixture over strong coffee. The result was thick, sweet, and surprisingly rich.

Born from shortage and ingenuity, egg coffee remains a beloved specialty. Vietnamese coffee reflects a culture that transforms limitation into creativity.

BOA BUÔN

SWEDEN
FIKA AND THE PAUSE

Three cups rest on small saucers. Cinnamon buns sit in the center of the table, their spirals soft and sugared. Hands wrap around warm mugs as conversation moves easily from one voice to another. In Sweden, coffee is woven into *fika*.

Fika is more than a coffee break. It is a pause built into the rhythm of the day. At work, at home, or in a café, people step away from tasks and sit together. The point is not speed. It is presence.

Coffee is usually paired with something sweet. A cinnamon bun, a pastry, a simple cookie. What matters is that the moment is shared. Hierarchies soften. Phones are set aside. Laughter replaces deadlines.

Fika is often planned, not squeezed in. It signals that rest and connection are not distractions from productivity, but part of it.

Coffee arrived in Sweden in the 17th century and quickly gained popularity. In the 18th century, King Gustav III believed coffee was harmful and banned it. An experiment meant to prove its dangers reportedly failed, and the bans eventually faded. The coffee did not.

Over time, the tradition of fika developed as a regular social pause, reflecting broader Swedish values of balance and community. Today, fika remains an essential part of daily life across the country.

Fira CAFÉ

CHINA
COFFEE AND THE MOUNTAIN HARVEST

Morning light spreads across the terraced hills.

Coffee plants grow along the slopes, their branches heavy with red cherries. Pickers move carefully between the rows, baskets resting against their backs as they gather the ripest fruit by hand.

Much of the country's coffee is grown in Yunnan province, where altitude, rainfall, and volcanic soil create favorable conditions for cultivation. Farms stretch across valleys and hillsides, and harvesting follows the rhythm of the seasons. Each cherry is collected carefully. Later, the beans are washed, dried, and sorted before beginning their journey beyond the fields.

What begins on these quiet slopes eventually travels far beyond the valleys. In China, coffee connects distant mountain farms with a rapidly changing modern culture.

Coffee first reached China through foreign trade during the 19th century, but it remained relatively uncommon for many decades in a society long shaped by tea traditions. Large-scale cultivation began in Yunnan province during the late 20th century, where climate and elevation proved well suited for Arabica coffee. Production expanded steadily, and Yunnan coffee is now exported around the world.

At the same time, coffee consumption has grown rapidly in Chinese cities. Cafés, specialty roasters, and international chains have helped introduce new brewing styles and coffee traditions to a younger generation.

Today, China's coffee story stretches from mountain farms to bustling urban cafés, reflecting a culture where old traditions and new habits coexist.

MEXICO
COFFEE AND CLAY

The pot sits on the stove, cinnamon drifting through the air.

Coffee simmers slowly with *piloncillo**, the unrefined cane sugar that melts into deep caramel sweetness. A stick of cinnamon rolls gently in the heat. The scent carries before the first cup is poured.

In Mexico, coffee is often brewed in a clay pot called an *olla*. The clay tempers the heat and lends a faint earthiness to the brew. Cups are filled generously. The coffee is warm, sweet, and lightly spiced.

It is served in kitchens and on patios, early in the morning or late into the evening. Pan dulce rests nearby. Conversation unfolds easily, carried by the sweetness in the cup.

The clay, spice, and sugar turn coffee into something shared and familiar.
This is coffee that comforts.

A SIP OF HISTORY

Coffee arrived in Mexico during the colonial period, introduced through Spanish trade routes. Over time, it merged with local ingredients and traditions. Indigenous communities adapted the brew to their own kitchens, incorporating piloncillo and native clay cookware. The clay olla and the use of cinnamon reflect a blending of European trade goods and regional flavors. Café de olla became not just a drink, but a meeting point between cultures, shaped by both colonial exchange and local identity.

*Unrefined cane sugar is commonly used in Mexico and parts of Latin America. It is made by boiling fresh sugarcane juice until it thickens, then pouring it into molds where it hardens into solid cones or blocks.

YEMEN
COFFEE AND MOUNTAINS OF MOCHA

High in Yemen's terraced mountains, coffee plants cling to steep hillsides carved by hand over centuries. Stone walls trace the contours of the land. The air is dry, the light sharp. Here, coffee took root not just as a crop, but as a tradition shaped by terrain and devotion.

By the 15th century, coffee was cultivated intentionally in Yemen. Sufi monks brewed it to remain awake through long nights of prayer. From the mountains, coffee traveled down to the port city of Mocha, where it entered global trade. For generations, coffee bound for Europe passed through this Red Sea harbor, carrying Yemen's name across continents.

Coffee in Yemen is served carefully, often in small cups. It signals welcome and respect. Alongside brewed coffee, there is *qishr*, a lighter drink made from dried coffee husks, ginger, and sometimes cinnamon. Aromatic and gently spiced, it reflects a preference for warmth over intensity.

Early coffeehouses flourished here as well, becoming places of discussion, learning, and social exchange. Trade, faith, and conversation met at the same table.

A SIP OF HISTORY

For centuries, Yemen protected its coffee plants carefully. Exported beans were often boiled or partially roasted to prevent them from sprouting elsewhere. It was only in the 17th century that viable seeds were smuggled out, allowing coffee cultivation to spread to India, Indonesia, and eventually the Americas. Yemen's early control shaped the global geography of coffee for generations.

BOSNIA & HERZEGOVINA
COFFEE AND THE BRIDGE

Steam rises from the *džezva* as it is lifted carefully from the heat.

In Bosnia and Herzegovina, coffee is prepared with patience. Water is brought to a gentle boil before finely ground coffee is added. The foam forms slowly. The pour is steady and deliberate.

Small porcelain cups rest on a round metal tray. A sugar cube waits on the side. Some dip it lightly before the first sip. Others let it dissolve slowly into the dark surface. The coffee is thick, settling quietly at the bottom of the cup.

The tray carries more than the cups it holds. It carries continuity. People sit. The first sip is taken. Conversation begins softly and gathers strength. Refills are uncommon. The cup is meant to be finished slowly.

Nearby, the old stone bridge arches over the river, holding its shape through centuries of change. The coffee is poured. The cup is lifted. The ritual continues.

A SIP OF HISTORY

Coffee reached Bosnia during centuries of Ottoman presence and became woven into daily life. Over time, the ritual evolved into Bosanska kafa, *reflecting local identity and pride.*

During the Siege of Sarajevo in the 1990s, coffee beans were scarce. People roasted barley and improvised substitutes rather than abandoning the ritual. Even when the drink changed, the gathering did not.

Through empire, change, and hardship, this tradition endured.

INDIA
FILTER COFFEE AND THE MORNING POUR

The coffee is poured from one metal tumbler to another, lifted high so it falls in a smooth, steady stream. The movement cools the liquid and builds a light foam on top. Often, chicory is blended in to give the coffee greater body, and the aroma is rich and nutty.

In parts of southern India, the day begins like this.

Finely ground coffee brews slowly in a metal filter, the *decoction** collecting below. Hot milk is added generously. Sugar dissolves quickly. The final pour between the tumbler and the *dabarah* is both practical and practiced.

Mornings gather around this sound. Newspapers are opened. Shop shutters rise. Conversations begin. The first cup is strong and sweet, meant to awaken rather than linger. The ritual is brief but deliberate, repeated daily.

In India, coffee does not stretch into the afternoon. It sets the day in motion.

Coffee is believed to have reached India in the 17th century. According to legend, a Sufi saint named Baba Budan smuggled seven coffee beans out of Yemen by strapping them to his chest and planting them in the hills of Karnataka. From those first plants, cultivation spread across southern India.

Over time, local preferences shaped the drink. Chicory was added for body, and the metal filter became central to preparation. What began as a secret carried across borders has become a morning ritual woven into daily life.

*Decoction is a concentrated liquid made by extracting flavor or soluble compounds from a substance through brewing or boiling.

KAAPI
AN FOOD
MASALA

IRELAND
COFFEE AND THE WARMTH AFTER

The glass is warmed first.

Freshly brewed coffee is sweetened. Irish whiskey follows and is stirred gently through.
A layer of lightly whipped cream is floated carefully on top, thick enough to hold its shape,
soft enough to sip through.

The drink is not stirred again.

In Ireland, people often prepare Irish coffee after dinner, on a long journey, or when the weather
presses in from the Atlantic. The contrast is deliberate: hot coffee below, cool cream above.
Held in both hands, the glass offers warmth before the first taste. Each sip moves through the
cool cream before reaching the strong coffee beneath.

The contrast defines it: heat and chill, strength and softness. The room grows quieter. Glass rests
on a wooden counter. Someone tells a story that grows better with each sip and each retelling.

Irish coffee does not start the day. It belongs to the evening, to conversation that lingers,
and rough weather kept just outside the door.

*Irish coffee is said to have been created in the 1940s at Foynes Airbase, when a chef named
Joe Sheridan added whiskey to coffee to warm weary travelers. When asked if it was Brazilian
coffee, he reportedly replied, "No, it's Irish coffee."*

*The drink gained international recognition after being introduced to the United States, and it
remains closely associated with Irish hospitality.*

WHISKY

Coffee Traditions

Around The World

CAFÉ SHAHOR!

OMANI QAHWA
HOSPITALITY & RESPECT

AHLA WA SAHLAN! ENJOY COFFEE!
KAWA TRADITION!

THE JEBENA: A TRADITION
امانيا
اخوان
اعائلة

GERMANY
KAFFEEKLATSCH AND CONVERSATION

The coffee is poured just as the cake is sliced.

A Bundt cake sits in the center of the table, dusted lightly with powdered sugar and ready to be shared. A layered *Torte* waits nearby. Porcelain cups clink against saucers. Someone passes a bowl of *Schlagsahne*, sweetened whipped cream that crowns many German cakes. Plates are filled generously.

In Germany, *Kaffeeklatsch* brings families, friends, and generations together.

The special porcelain set is brought out for guests, sometimes the same one that grandmother once used. Freshly brewed filter coffee steams in the cups. A spoon dips into the *Schlagsahne* again. Plates are replenished without ceremony. The conversation moves easily from exchanging recipes to family news to neighborhood stories.

This ritual often unfolds in the afternoon, when the day begins to slow. Neighbors drop by. Children play nearby. The coffee pot stays within reach.

Kaffeeklatsch marks birthdays and ordinary Wednesdays alike. It turns a simple afternoon into something familiar and unmistakably German.

A SIP OF HISTORY

As coffee became more accessible in German households during the 18th and 19th centuries, the afternoon coffee table grew in popularity. What began as an occasional indulgence evolved into a regular social custom centered around coffee and Kuchen.

Kaffeeklatsch remains a defining tradition of German hospitality.

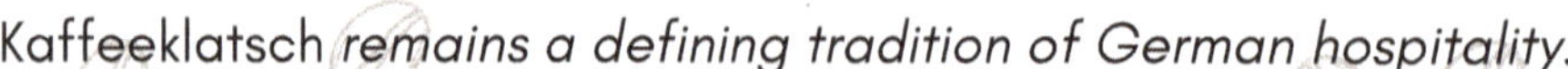

©Bibi LeBlanc/Culture.to.Color®

INDONESIA
KOPI AND THE DEPTH OF THE GLASS

Hot water is poured directly over finely ground coffee. There is no filter, no separation. The coffee rests as the grounds slowly sink and the surface begins to clear.

This preparation, known as *kopi tubruk*, is one of the most recognizable ways coffee is brewed across the archipelago. Finely ground coffee is mixed with hot water and allowed to settle naturally before drinking.

The first sips are taken slowly as the coffee clears. The flavor is full and earthy. Before the final sip, some tap the side of the glass gently to settle the remaining grounds. The last mouthful is taken carefully, leaving the sediment behind.

Coffee drinking in Indonesia is woven into everyday life in homes, roadside stalls, and small neighborhood cafés known as *warung kopi*. Coffee conversations unfold during morning routines, work breaks, and quiet moments throughout the day.

Across the islands, coffee grows in volcanic soil shaped by altitude and humidity. Regions such as Sumatra, Java, and Sulawesi are known for distinctive coffees with their rich body and fruity notes.

A SIP OF HISTORY

In the late 17th century, Dutch traders introduced coffee plants from Arabia to the island of Java. There, in the fertile volcanic soil, coffee was cultivated on a large scale for the first time outside its original home.

From Java, the beans were shipped to Europe, where they quickly gained popularity. The name Java became synonymous with coffee itself, reflecting Indonesia's lasting role in shaping the global coffee map.

TORA
BIKA

ISRAEL
COFFEE AT THE SHARED TABLE

The coffee simmers slowly in a small metal pot.

Warm flatbread rests in a woven basket. Bowls of olives glisten with olive oil. Eggs sit beside creamy dips swirled with herbs and tahini. Dates and small dishes gather in the center, passed easily from hand to hand.

In Israel, coffee rarely arrives alone.

Traditional *café botz* is brewed thick and unfiltered, poured into small glasses where the grounds settle at the bottom. The flavor is strong and direct. It is sipped between bites, between stories, between debates.

Breakfast stretches comfortably into late morning. Conversations overlap. Plates are refilled. Someone pours more coffee without asking.

Across the country, coffee culture moves between tradition and modern café life. Espresso machines hum in busy city streets, while small pots still simmer in kitchens and markets.

A SIP OF HISTORY

Coffee reached the region during Ottoman rule and became embedded in daily life long before modern borders existed. In the 20th century, waves of immigration introduced European espresso traditions alongside longstanding Middle Eastern brewing styles.

Together, these traditions created a coffee culture that reflects the country's layered history and many cultural roots.

OMAN
COFFEE AND THE DALLAH

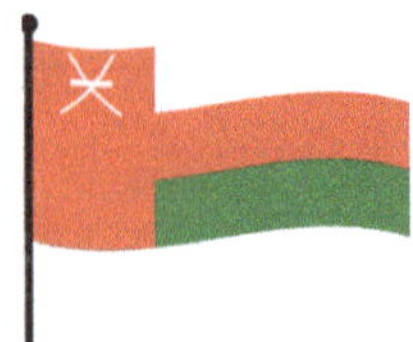

The *dallah* tilts gently as coffee is poured.

A thin stream fills the small cups waiting on the tray. The coffee is pale in color, lightly roasted, and scented with cardamom. Dates sit beside the cups, their delicate sweetness balancing the bitterness of the drink.

In Oman, guests are offered a cup soon after entering a home. The host pours carefully, filling each cup only partway. The gesture is modest but attentive. The cup is accepted with the right hand and finished in a few quiet sips. Refills follow without asking. When a guest has had enough, the small cup is gently shaken before it is returned to the host.

The cups remain small. The pours remain measured. Conversation unfolds slowly around the tray. The host lifts the *dallah* again and again, each pour marking the rhythm of hospitality.

In Oman, coffee is first a gesture of welcome.

A SIP OF HISTORY

For centuries, Oman stood at the crossroads of maritime trade routes linking East Africa, Arabia, and South Asia. Along these routes, coffee became part of a ritual of welcome shared across the Arabian Peninsula.

Omani coffee, known as kahwa, developed its own distinctive character. The beans are lightly roasted and often flavored with cardamom, then poured from a traditional metal pot called a dallah into small handleless cups. Serving coffee to guests became a symbol of respect and generosity, a custom that remains central to Omani hospitality today.

COSTA RICA
COFFEE AND PURA VIDA

Morning light moves across the hills where coffee plants grow in neat rows along volcanic slopes, their red cherries bright against deep green leaves. Pickers move carefully between branches, selecting only what is ready.

In Costa Rica, coffee is tied to the land.

Harvesting is done by hand. The beans are washed, dried, and sorted with steady attention. Many farms are small and family-run, passed down through generations. The work is seasonal but constant, shaped by the climate, altitude, and soil.

Later, the coffee is brewed strong and clean, often through a *chorreador*, a simple wooden stand holding a cloth filter. The method is uncomplicated. The flavor is clear and balanced. Coffee is served at breakfast and again in the afternoon, offered without formality. It accompanies conversation, but it also reflects something broader.

¡Pura Vida!

Pura Vida is a way of living, where life is taken as it comes and appreciated as it is. In Costa Rica, *Pura Vida* is found in the everyday, in the pause, the cup, and the moment shared.

Coffee arrived in Costa Rica in the late 18th century and quickly took root in the country's rich volcanic soil. By the 19th century, it had become one of the nation's most important exports, shaping trade routes and daily life.

Known as grano de oro, or "the golden bean," coffee helped define Costa Rica's identity, a legacy that continues in every cup today.

LEBANON
Coffee And The Art Of Staying

The pot rests on low heat. The foam rises gently. Someone watches carefully so it does not spill.

In Lebanon, coffee often arrives at the beginning of a visit. It is strong and dark, often scented lightly with cardamom. Guests are offered coffee as soon as they sit down. To refuse is rare. To accept is to enter the rhythm of the home. Served in small cups, it invites slow sipping.

Coffee accompanies serious discussions and light gossip alike. It appears at celebrations and during mourning. The ritual does not shift with the mood of the room. The host pours. The guest receives, and the conversation deepens gradually.

Stories unfold in layers. A second cup may follow. Sometimes the empty cup is turned upside down, the remaining grounds forming patterns that invite interpretation.

No one measures time too closely; sharing coffee allows people to stay. To speak openly. To strengthen the ties that hold families and friends together.

In Lebanon, coffee does not wait for the right moment. It creates it.

Coffee reached Lebanon during Ottoman rule and became firmly embedded in everyday life. Over centuries, the preparation and serving style developed into a deeply rooted expression of hospitality.

The small cups, careful pours, and unhurried pace reflect traditions of respect and welcome that remain central to Lebanese culture today.

SUDAN
COFFEE AND THE GATHERING

The charcoal glows low. The pan rests above it.

Green beans roast slowly, stirred by hand as the aroma spreads through the air. The scent draws people closer. Someone adjusts the heat. Someone else arranges the cups.

In Sudan, the beans are ground by hand. The roasting happens in view of everyone present. Spices such as ginger or cardamom may be added, giving the brew warmth and depth. The coffee is poured into small cups and passed carefully from one guest to the next.

Sometimes incense is burned beside the coffee, adding another layer of fragrance to the gathering. The ceremony is often led by women, who guide the preparation with steady hands. Conversation flows easily. Laughter rises. Neighbors join without invitation.

The ritual is not hurried, but it is lively. Coffee here marks welcome and belonging.
It fills space with scent before it fills the cup.

In Sudan, the gathering forms around the flame.

A SIP OF HISTORY

Sudan's coffee tradition predates borders and modern definitions of coffee culture. Coffee reached Sudan through trade networks connecting the Horn of Africa with the Arabian Peninsula.

Rooted in ancient practices, Sudanese coffee is deeply ceremonial, richly spiced, and closely tied to community gatherings, storytelling, and respect for ancestry. Here, coffee is not only a beverage. It is a cultural expression passed down through generations in both rural villages and urban neighborhoods.

THAILAND
COFFEE AND THE HIGHLAND HARVEST

Morning mist lingers over the northern hills.

Coffee plants grow along steep mountain slopes, their leaves dark against the lighter greens of surrounding forests. Nearby, beans dry on woven trays while others roast slowly over a small flame.

In Thailand, coffee begins in the northern highlands. Cooler mountain climates in regions such as Chiang Mai and Chiang Rai allow arabica coffee to grow along forested slopes. Many farms are small and community-run, where harvesting, drying, and roasting remain closely tied to daily life. The work follows the seasons' rhythm. Cherries are handpicked, carefully sorted, and prepared for roasting.

From these hills, the beans travel south toward towns and cities. There, coffee often appears as Thai iced coffee. Street vendors brew strong coffee through a cloth sock filter, pouring it into metal containers before mixing it with ice and sweetened condensed milk.

The result is a drink that is bold, sweet, and instantly refreshing in the tropical heat.

A SIP OF HISTORY

Coffee cultivation expanded in Thailand during the 20th century, particularly in the mountainous north where climate and elevation support arabica production. Government programs encouraged farmers to grow coffee as an alternative crop, helping establish new agricultural communities in the region.

At the same time, coffee developed its own urban identity and today, Thailand's coffee culture connects mountain farms, busy markets, and a growing specialty café scene.

SOMALIA
COFFEE, SPICE, AND SOCIAL CONNECTION

A guest arrives, and the offer of coffee is part of the greeting.

The pot rests near the coals. Small cups are set out almost immediately.

The drink, known locally as *qaxwo*, is brewed strongly and often scented with spices such as cardamom, cinnamon, cloves, or ginger. The preparation itself is simple, but the gesture carries meaning. The coffee pot passes easily from hand to hand, a quiet reminder of the long trading connections between the Horn of Africa and the Arabian Peninsula.

Guests settle onto mats or cushions as the host pours the coffee into small cups. Conversation unfolds slowly, moving easily between family news, local stories, and everyday concerns. Unlike the formal coffee ceremonies found in some neighboring cultures, Somali coffee gatherings are relaxed and fluid. What matters is not ritual, but presence.

Coffee here is less about the drink itself than the moment it creates.

For centuries, coffee has traveled through the Horn of Africa along trade routes linking East Africa and the Arabian Peninsula. While Ethiopia is widely recognized as coffee's birthplace, neighboring regions, including Somalia, developed their own traditions shaped by commerce, migration, and cultural exchange.

In Somalia, the word qaxwo reflects these connections, deriving from the Arabic word for coffee. Over time, local customs added their own character to the drink, particularly the use of aromatic spices. Today, serving coffee remains a meaningful act of hospitality.

JAPAN
COFFEE AND ATTENTION

The kettle hums softly.

Water is poured in a slow, steady circle over freshly ground coffee. The bloom rises, then settles. The pour pauses. Begins again. Nothing spills. Nothing is rushed.

In Japan, coffee is an act of attention.

Each step is deliberate. The grind is measured carefully. The water temperature matters. The timing of each pour matters, and the barista watches closely as the filter drips into a waiting cup. Silence is part of the experience.

In traditional *kissaten** and modern specialty cafés alike, coffee is brewed with care and served without spectacle. The cup is placed gently before the guest.

Conversation, if it comes, remains soft. Coffee here does not compete for attention. It rewards it.

Coffee arrived in Japan in the 19th century through international trade, but gained broader popularity in the 20th century. Traditional kissaten coffee houses developed their own meticulous brewing standards long before the global specialty coffee movement emerged.

Japan is known worldwide for precision brewing techniques and a deep respect for craftsmanship.

*a traditional Japanese coffee shop.

喫茶店

CUBA
CAFÉ CUBANO AND THE CORNER

The espresso is brewed strong and sweet.

Sugar is whipped with the first drops of coffee until the mixture turns pale and creamy. The rest of the espresso is poured over it, forming a thick, caramel-colored foam called *espuma* on top. The cups are small. The flavor is not.

A single brew, called a colada, often becomes several small servings. Tiny cups are filled and passed across the counter. Someone takes a sip and hands it back. At the corner, people pause, talk, and share the small cups. Conversations spill into the street. The coffee is quick, but the energy lingers.

This is *Café Cubano*. Bold. Sweet. Direct.

It is taken in the morning before work, in the afternoon between errands, and in the evening when the air cools. Someone always seems to be brewing another round.

The cigar, the cup, the street — each holds its place.

In Cuba, coffee does not stand alone. It belongs to the moment around it.

Coffee arrived in Cuba in the 18th century and flourished under Spanish influence. The island became a major coffee producer, especially in the eastern regions. Over time, Café Cubano developed its distinct preparation method, blending strong espresso with whipped sugar.

Today, the tradition remains central to Cuban social life, both on the island and in Cuban communities abroad.

ABOUT THE AUTHOR

Bibi LeBlanc is an international speaker, entrepreneur, and world traveler with a deep passion for storytelling and building community. She has always been drawn to stories, especially those that weave people and places together. Growing up in West Berlin during the Cold War profoundly shaped her outlook and nurtured her appreciation for connection and culture.

Her curiosity has carried her from skydiving adventures to journeys across continents, always noticing the small details that give each place its own pulse. Those experiences often find their way into her work with Culture to Color®, where she turns real stories, complex concepts, and ideas into Explainer Books™ that invite readers to slow down, explore, and discover the world through creativity, imagination, and color.

Coffee Traditions Around the World grew from that same spirit. While traveling, no matter where she went, people gathered around coffee. In busy cities and quiet villages, in elegant cafés and modest kitchens, coffee was rarely just a drink. It was a pause, a ritual, an invitation to conversation. This book celebrates those shared moments and the cultural stories that rise gently from every cup.

When she is not immersed in a new book project, she may be planning her next adventure, chatting with strangers who quickly become friends, or enjoying a quiet cup of coffee somewhere that feels a little like home.

Every project she creates carries a touch of her own journey and often sparks a fresh sense of wonder in those who read her work.

ONE LAST CUP

I hope you enjoyed traveling the world with me, one cup at a time.

In my travels, I've found that coffee connects. It is a constant, even as it appears in many different forms and preparations.

I've had many a cup as I created this book, each one a small reminder of the moments coffee makes possible.

From my work desk to lively cafés, from simple routines to meaningful rituals, coffee creates space for people to come together, talk, reflect, or simply sit side by side.

The details may change from place to place. The purpose rarely does.

Wherever you are, however you take your coffee, I hope it brings you a moment to slow down, to connect, and to simply be.

Thank you for joining me on this journey!

Bibi Le Blanc

P.S. I would love to see your colored creations. You can share them with me
bibi@culturetocolor.com
Seeing your interpretations brings these traditions
to life in the most beautiful way.

OTHER BOOKS

culturetocolor.com/shop

BY BIBI LEBLANC

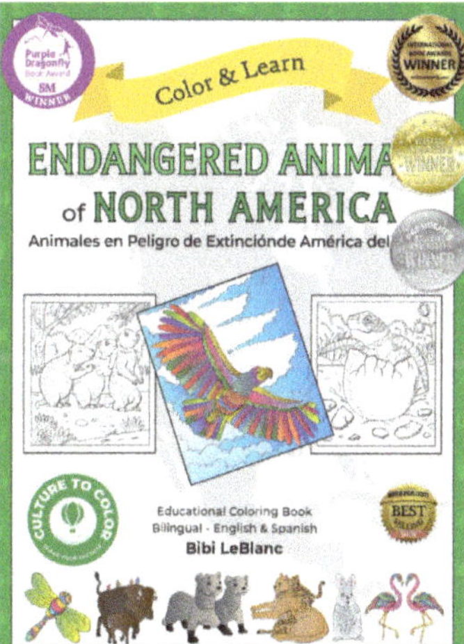

BOOK AWARDS

This book was created by Bibi LeBlanc, a best-selling author and the winner of the

Chanticleer International Book Award
Human Relations Indie Book Award
Next Generation International Indie Book Award
FAPA President's Book Award
International Book Award
& Finalist in the Eric Hoffer International Book Award
Wings of Freedom - The Story of the Berlin Airlift
*

New York City Big Book Award
International Book Award
FAPA President's Book Award
Berlin Divided - Berlin United
*

Kops-Fetherling International Book Award for
Discover Food & Wine of Tuscany, Italy
*

Purple Dragonfly International Book Award
2022 International Book Award
IBPA Benjamin Franklin Book Award
FAPA President's Book Award
Endangered Animals of North America
*

Next Generation International Indie Book Award
Purple Dragonfly International Book Award
New York City Big Book Award
FAPA President's Book Award
Explore the Sights of San Francisco, Chinatown

BENEFITS OF COLORING

If you include coloring in your daily routine, you will find
it has many benefits for you, the coloring artist.
To name just a few, coloring can:

IMPROVE FOCUS

Coloring requires repetition and attention to detail. It opens up
your brain's frontal lobe, which controls organizing and
problem-solving, and allows you to focus on the activity
rather than your worries.

REDUCE STRESS AND ANXIETY

Coloring relaxes your brain's fear center (amygdala), putting you
in a state similar to meditation. Coloring helps remove
irritating thoughts and allows the creative mind to run free and relax.

IMPROVE SLEEP

Coloring as a bedtime ritual - instead of using electronics -
can lead to a better night's sleep. The light emitted by electronic devices
lowers the level of melatonin, your sleep hormone,
whereas coloring does not affect your melatonin level.

You can take coloring supplies anywhere.
And you don't have to be an artist or an expert to color
and create something beautiful.
Seeing your finished coloring page provides
a sense of accomplishment.

Tag us with your colored pages and #CultureToColor

DID YOU KNOW...?

THE PLANT & BEANS

- Coffee beans are actually the seeds of a fruit, often called a coffee cherry.
- There are over 100 species of coffee plants, but most of the world drinks just two: Arabica and Robusta.
- A coffee tree can live over 50 years.
- It takes about 2,000 coffee cherries to make one pound of roasted coffee.
- Coffee grows best in a specific band around the world called the "Coffee Belt."

SCIENCE & SURPRISES

- Coffee doesn't give you energy, it blocks the chemical that makes you feel tired.
- The effect of caffeine usually begins within 15–30 minutes.
- Coffee contains hundreds of aromatic compounds, which is why it smells so complex.
- Light roast coffee actually has slightly more caffeine than dark roast (by volume).
- The smell of coffee alone can make people feel more alert, even before drinking it.

FUN & UNEXPECTED

- Finland drinks more coffee per person than any other country.
- Coffee is one of the most traded commodities in the world.
- Espresso has less caffeine per serving than drip coffee, but it's more concentrated.
- Decaf coffee still contains a small amount of caffeine.
- Used coffee grounds can be reused as fertilizer, deodorizer, or even natural scrub.

www.ingramcontent.com/pod-product-compliance
Lightning Source LLC
Chambersburg PA
CBHW040857070726

47599CB00035B/2031